O'Connor

by Iain Gray

GW00775669

PUBLISHING

WRITING *to* REMEMBER

LangSyne
PUBLISHING
WRITING *to* REMEMBER

79 Main Street, Newtongrange,
Midlothian EH22 4NA
Tel: 0131 344 0414   Fax: 0845 075 6085
E-mail: info@lang-syne.co.uk
www.langsyneshop.co.uk

Design by Dorothy Meikle
Printed by Printwell Ltd
© Lang Syne Publishers Ltd 2016

ISBN 978-1-85217-303-6

O'Connor

MOTTO:
From God comes every help.

CREST:
A mailed arm, with the hand holding
a sword entwined with a serpent.

NAME variations include:
Ó Conchobhair (Gaelic)
Ó Concubain (Gaelic)
O'Conor
O'Conner
Conners
Conor
Connors

Chapter one:
Origins of Irish surnames

According to an old saying, there are two types of Irish – those who actually are Irish and those who wish they were.

This sentiment is only one example of the allure that the high romance and drama of the proud nation's history holds for thousands of people scattered across the world today.

It's a sad fact, however, that the vast majority of Irish surnames are found far beyond Irish shores, rather than on the Emerald Isle itself.

The population stood at around eight million souls in 1841, but today it stands at fewer than six million.

This is mainly a tragic consequence of the potato famine, also known as the Great Hunger, which devastated Ireland between 1845 and 1849.

The Irish peasantry had become almost wholly reliant for basic sustenance on the potato, first introduced from the Americas in the seventeenth century.

When the crop was hit by a blight, at least 800,000 people starved to death while an estimated two million others were forced to seek a new life far from their native shores – particularly in America, Canada, and Australia.

The effects of the potato blight continued until about 1851, by which time a firm pattern of emigration had become established.

Ireland's loss, however, was to the gain of the countries in which the immigrants settled, contributing enormously, as their descendants do today, to the well being of the nations in which their forefathers settled.

But those who were forced through dire circumstance to establish a new life in foreign parts never forgot their roots, or the proud heritage and traditions of the land that gave them birth.

Nor do their descendants.

It is a heritage that is inextricably bound up in the colourful variety of Irish names themselves – and the origin and history of these names forms an integral part of the vibrant drama that is the nation's history, one of both glorious fortune and tragic misfortune.

This history is well documented, and one of the most important and fascinating of the earliest sources are *The Annals of the Four Masters*, compiled between 1632 and 1636 by four friars at the Franciscan Monastery in County Donegal.

Compiled from earlier sources, and purporting to go back to the Biblical Deluge, much of the material takes in the mythological origins and history of Ireland and the Irish.

This includes tales of successive waves of invaders and settlers such as the Fomorians, the Partholonians, the Nemedians, the Fir Bolgs, the Tuatha De Danann, and the Laigain.

Of particular interest are the *Milesian Genealogies*,

because the majority of Irish clans today claim a descent from either Heremon, Ir, or Heber – three of the sons of Milesius, a king of what is now modern day Spain.

These sons invaded Ireland in the second millennium B.C, apparently in fulfilment of a mysterious prophecy received by their father.

This Milesian lineage is said to have ruled Ireland for nearly 3,000 years, until the island came under the sway of England's King Henry II in 1171 following what is known as the Cambro-Norman invasion.

This is an important date not only in Irish history in general, but for the effect the invasion subsequently had for Irish surnames.

'Cambro' comes from the Welsh, and 'Cambro-Norman' describes those Welsh knights of Norman origin who invaded Ireland.

But they were invaders who stayed, inter-marrying with the native Irish population and founding their own proud dynasties that bore Cambro-Norman names such as Archer, Barbour, Brannagh, Fitzgerald, Fitzgibbon, Fleming, Joyce, Plunkett, and Walsh – to name only a few.

These 'Cambro-Norman' surnames that still flourish throughout the world today form one of the three main categories in which Irish names can be placed – those of Gaelic-Irish, Cambro-Norman, and Anglo-Irish.

Previous to the Cambro-Norman invasion of the twelfth century, and throughout the earlier invasions and settlement of those wild bands of sea rovers known as the Vikings in the eighth and ninth centuries, the population of the island was relatively small, and it was normal for a person to be identified through the use of only a forename.

But as population gradually increased and there were many more people with the same forename, surnames were adopted to distinguish one person, or one community, from another.

Individuals identified themselves with their own particular tribe, or 'tuath', and this tribe – that also became known as a clann, or clan – took its name from some distinguished ancestor who had founded the clan.

The Gaelic-Irish form of the name Kelly, for example, is Ó Ceallaigh, or O'Kelly, indicating descent from an original 'Ceallaigh', with the 'O' denoting 'grandson of.' The name was later anglicised to Kelly.

The prefix 'Mac' or 'Mc', meanwhile, as with the clans of the Scottish Highlands, denotes 'son of.'

Although the Irish clans had much in common with their Scottish counterparts, one important difference lies in what are known as 'septs', or branches, of the clan.

Septs of Scottish clans were groups who often bore an entirely different name from the clan name but were under the clan's protection.

In Ireland, septs were groups that shared the same name and who could be found scattered throughout the four provinces of Ulster, Leinster, Munster, and Connacht.

The 'golden age' of the Gaelic-Irish clans, infused as their veins were with the blood of Celts, pre-dates the Viking invasions of the eighth and ninth centuries and the Norman invasion of the twelfth century, and the sacred heart of the country was the Hill of Tara, near the River Boyne, in County Meath.

Known in Gaelic as 'Teamhar na Rí', or Hill of Kings, it was the royal seat of the 'Ard Rí Éireann', or High King of Ireland, to whom the petty kings, or chieftains, from the island's provinces were ultimately subordinate.

It was on the Hill of Tara, beside a stone pillar known as the Irish 'Lia Fáil', or Stone of Destiny, that the High Kings were inaugurated and, according to legend, this stone would emit a piercing screech that could be heard all over Ireland when touched by the hand of the rightful king.

The Hill of Tara is today one of the island's main tourist attractions.

Opposition to English rule over Ireland, established in the wake of the Cambro-Norman invasion, broke out frequently and the harsh solution adopted by the powerful forces of the Crown was to forcibly evict the native Irish from their lands.

These lands were then granted to Protestant colonists, or 'planters', from Britain.

Many of these colonists, ironically, came from Scotland and were the descendants of the original 'Scotti', or 'Scots', who gave their name to Scotland after migrating there in the fifth century A.D., from the north of Ireland.

Colonisation entailed harsh penal laws being imposed on the majority of the native Irish population, stripping them practically of all of their rights.

The Crown's main bastion in Ireland was Dublin and its environs, known as the Pale, and it was the dispossessed peasantry who lived outside this Pale, desperately striving to eke out a meagre living.

It was this that gave rise to the modern-day expression of someone or something being 'beyond the pale'.

Attempts were made to stamp out all aspects of the ancient Gaelic-Irish culture, to the extent that even to bear a Gaelic-Irish name was to invite discrimination.

This is why many Gaelic-Irish names were anglicised with, for example, and noted above, Ó Ceallaigh, or O'Kelly, being anglicised to Kelly.

Succeeding centuries have seen strong revivals of Gaelic-Irish consciousness, however, and this has led to many families reverting back to the original form of their name, while the language itself is frequently found on the fluent tongues of an estimated 90,000 to 145,000 of the island's population.

Ireland's turbulent history of religious and political strife is one that lasted well into the twentieth century, a landmark century that saw the partition of the island into the twenty-six counties of the independent Republic of

Ireland, or Eire, and the six counties of Northern Ireland, or Ulster.

Dublin, originally founded by Vikings, is now a vibrant and truly cosmopolitan city while the proud city of Belfast is one of the jewels in the crown of Ulster.

It was Saint Patrick who first brought the light of Christianity to Ireland in the fifth century A.D.

Interpretations of this Christian message have varied over the centuries, often leading to bitter sectarian conflict – but the many intricately sculpted Celtic Crosses found all over the island are symbolic of a unity that crosses the sectarian divide.

It is an image that fuses the 'old gods' of the Celts with Christianity.

All the signs from the early years of this new millennium indicate that sectarian strife may soon become a thing of the past – with the Irish and their many kinsfolk across the world, be they Protestant or Catholic, finding common purpose in the rich tapestry of their shared heritage.

Chapter two:
Last of the High Kings

With the exception of only a select few, there is arguably no other Irish clan that bestrides the pages of the nation's history to such an extent as the O'Connors.

Different septs, or branches, of the clan were to be found scattered across the island from earliest times – but what they all had in common was that their name derived from the personal name Conchobhar, or Conchobhair, indicating 'champion.'

It proved to be a truly apt designation as the different septs, all in their separate ways, stamped their marks on Ireland's colourful and turbulent tale.

Among the septs were the O'Connor Faly – with 'Faly' indicating the territory of Offaly – who claimed an illustrious descent from the celebrated Catháir Mór, who reigned as Ard Rí, or High King, from between 119 and 122A.D.

His reign ended in dramatic and bloody fashion at the hands of the gloriously named Conn Céthchathach, the Gaelic form for Conn of the Hundred Battles.

It was Conn of the Hundred Battles who attained the High Kingship after killing Catháir Mór at the battle of Moigh Acha, in present day Co. Meath.

There was also an O'Connor sept who flourished in present day Co. Kerry and whose stronghold for centuries was Carrigafoyle Castle, while the O'Connors of Corcomroe held sway in the north of the present day Co. Clare.

O'Connors were also to be found in the ancient province of Ulster, where they were known as the O'Connor Keenaght, but it was the O'Connors of the province of Connacht, recognised to this day as the 'Royal O'Connors', who became particularly prominent in the history of the Emerald Isle.

Indeed one source stated of the O'Connors in 1912 that: 'No family in Ireland claims greater antiquity and no family in Europe, royal or noble, can trace its descent through so many generations of legitimate ancestors.'

Split as they were into at least three septs of their own – the O'Connor Roe, O'Connor Sligo, and O'Connor Don – the genealogy of the O'Connors of Connacht is complex, but it is possible to disentangle the main strands.

This shows that apart from their own dominance as sub-kings of the province of Connacht they not only acted for a time as the Ard Rí, of Ireland as a whole, but also in effect represented the last of the ancient institution.

One of the most celebrated of these Ard Rí was the twelfth century Turlough Mor O'Conor, or O'Connor, who boasted no less than twenty children through three marriages, in addition to the building of a number of bridges and castles throughout his vast domains.

One of his most important legacies is the Irish national treasure known as the Cross of Cong, commissioned by him in about 1123 to carry what was considered to be a fragment of the 'True Cross' of Christ's crucifixion.

Sheathed in metal and decorated in bronze, silver, and gold, one of the inscriptions it carries is 'a prayer for Turlough Mor, King of Erin for whom this cross was made.'

It was one of his many sons, Rory O'Connor, who was destined to play a formative and ultimately tragic role in one of the most important episodes in his nation's history after taking over the mantle of the High Kingship following his father's death in 1156.

Twelfth century Ireland was far from being a unified nation, split up as it was into territories ruled over by squabbling chieftains who ruled as kings in their own right – and this inter-clan rivalry worked to the advantage of the invaders.

In a series of bloody conflicts one chieftain, or king, would occasionally gain the upper hand over his rivals, and by 1156 the most powerful was Muirchertach MacLochlainn, king of the powerful O'Neills.

He was opposed by the equally powerful Rory O'Connor, but he increased his power and influence by allying himself with Dermot MacMurrough, king of Leinster.

MacLochlainn and MacMurrough were aware that the main key to the kingdom of Ireland was the thriving trading port of Dublin that had been established by invading Vikings, or Ostmen, in 852 A.D.

Their combined forces took Dublin, but when MacLochlainn died the Dubliners rose up in revolt and overthrew the unpopular MacMurrough.

A triumphant Rory O'Connor now entered Dublin and was later inaugurated as Ard Rí, but MacMurrough was not one to humbly accept defeat.

He appealed for help from England's Henry II in unseating O'Connor, an act that was to radically affect the future course of Ireland's fortunes.

The English monarch agreed to help MacMurrough, but distanced himself from direct action by delegating his Norman subjects in Wales with the task.

These ambitious and battle-hardened barons and knights had first settled in Wales following the Norman Conquest of England in 1066 and, with an eye on rich booty, plunder, and lands, were only too eager to obey their sovereign's wishes and furnish MacMurrough with aid.

MacMurrough crossed the Irish Sea to Bristol, where he rallied powerful barons such as Robert Fitzstephen and Maurice Fitzgerald to his cause, along with Gilbert de Clare, Earl of Pembroke.

As an inducement to de Clare, MacMurrough offered him the hand of his beautiful young daughter, Aife, in marriage, with the further sweetener to the deal that he would take over the province of Leinster on MacMurrough's death.

The mighty Norman war machine soon moved into action, and so fierce and disciplined was their onslaught on the forces of Rory O'Connor and his allies that by 1170 they had re-captured Dublin, in the name of MacMurrough, and other strategically important territories.

Henry II now began to take cold feet over the venture, realising that he may have created a rival in the form of a separate Norman kingdom in Ireland.

Accordingly, he landed on the island, near Waterford, at the head of a large army in October of 1171 with the aim of curbing the power of his Cambro-Norman barons.

But protracted war between the king and his barons was averted when they submitted to the royal will, promising homage and allegiance in return for holding the territories they had conquered in the king's name.

Henry also received the submission and homage of many of the Irish chieftains, tired as they were with internecine warfare and also perhaps realising that as long as they were rivals and not united they were no match for the powerful forces the English Crown could muster.

English dominion over Ireland was ratified through the Treaty of Windsor of 1175, under the terms of which Rory O'Connor, for example, was only allowed to rule territory unoccupied by the Normans in the role of a vassal of the king.

This humiliation appears to have been too much for the proud Rory O'Connor to bear, for he abdicated his kingship and took himself off to monastic seclusion.

He died in 1198, the last in a line of no less than eleven O'Connor High Kings of Ireland.

Chapter three:

Keeping the faith

Rory O'Connor was succeeded in the kingship of Connacht by his half brother Cathal Crovedearg, better known as Charles of the Wine Red Hand, while a number of other O'Connors would also hold the province's kingship until the final suppression of the ancient Gaelic order.

These included Felim O'Connor, who was killed at the second battle of Athenry in 1316, while in command of a native Irish army thought to have numbered just under 3,000 men.

Felim's battle had been waged against English colonists, as had been those of his predecessors – one of whom is recorded in the annals as having attacked the province of Leinster with his army in 1187.

The annals state: 'He burned and demolished the castle of Kildare, where not one of the English escaped, but were all suffocated, or otherwise killed.

'They carried away their accoutrements, arms, shields, coats of mail, and horses, and slew two knights.'

Bullintubber Castle, in Castlerea, in present day Co. Roscommon, was for centuries the main stronghold of the O'Connors of Connacht, and it was this family who were responsible for the foundation of a number of abbeys that included Ballintubber Abbey and Roscommon Abbey.

But despite the number of abbeys and churches that graced the Irish landscape, the island was far from peaceful.

It was frequently torn apart by rebellion as the power of the English Crown and waves of colonists encroached further on the native Irish way of life.

A policy of 'plantation', or settlement of loyal Protestants in Ireland, had been started during the reign from 1491 to 1547 of Henry VIII, whose Reformation effectively outlawed the established Roman Catholic faith throughout his dominions.

In an insurrection that exploded in 1641, at least 2,000 Protestant settlers were massacred at the hands of Catholic landowners and their kinsfolk, while thousands more were driven from the lands they had acquired.

Terrible as the atrocities were against the Protestant settlers, subsequent accounts became greatly exaggerated, serving to fuel a burning desire on the part of Protestants for revenge against the rebels.

This revenge became directed not only against the rebels, but native Irish Catholics such as the O'Connors in general.

The English Civil War intervened to prevent immediate action, but following the execution of Charles I in 1649 and the consolidation of the power of England's Oliver Cromwell, the time was ripe was revenge.

The Lord Protector, as he was named, descended on Ireland at the head of a 20,000-strong army that landed at

Ringford, near Dublin, in August of 1649, and the consequences of this Cromwellian conquest still resonate throughout the island today.

He had three main aims: to quash all forms of rebellion, to 'remove' all Catholic landowners who had taken part in the rebellion, and to convert the native Irish to the Protestant faith.

An early warning of the terrors that were in store for the native Catholic Irish came when the town of Drogheda was stormed and taken in September and between 2,000 and 4,000 of its inhabitants killed, including priests who were summarily put to the sword.

The defenders of Drogheda's St. Peter's Church, who had refused to surrender, were burned to death as they huddled for refuge in the steeple and the church was deliberately torched.

A similar fate awaited Wexford, on the southeast coast, when at least 1,500 of its inhabitants were slaughtered, including 200 defenceless women, despite their pathetic pleas for mercy.

Cromwell soon held the land in a grip of iron, allowing him to implement what amounted to a policy of ethnic cleansing.

His troopers were given free rein to hunt down and kill priests, while what remained of Catholic estates such as those of the O'Connors were confiscated.

An edict was issued stating that any native Irish found

east of the River Shannon after May 1, 1654, faced either summary execution or transportation to the West Indies.

What proved to be the final death knell of families such as the O'Connors was sounded in 1688 following what was known as the Glorious Revolution.

This involved the flight into exile of the Catholic monarch James II (James VII of Scotland) and the accession to the throne of the Protestant William of Orange and his wife Mary.

Followers of James were known as Jacobites, and the O'Connors were prominent among those Jacobites who took up the sword in defence of not only the Stuart monarchy but also their religion.

In what is known as the War of the Two Kings, or the Williamite War, Ireland became the battleground for the attempt by Jacobites to restore James to his throne.

Key events from this period are still marked annually with marches and celebrations in Northern Ireland – most notably the lifting of the siege of Derry, or Londonderry, by Williamite forces in 1689 and the Williamite victory at the battle of the Boyne the following year.

The Jacobite defeat was finally ratified through the signing of the Treaty of Limerick in 1691.

What followed was the virtual destruction of the ancient Gaelic way of life of clans such as the O'Connors, when a serious of measures known as the Penal Laws were put into effect.

Under their terms Catholics were barred from the legal profession, the armed forces, and parliament, not allowed to bear arms or own a horse worth more than £5, barred from running their own schools, and from sending their children abroad for their education.

All Roman Catholic clergy and bishops were officially 'banished' from the island in 1697, while it has been estimated that by 1703 less than 15% of the land throughout the entire island was owned by Irish Catholics.

Faced with this oppression many Irish Catholics sought new lives abroad, while others converted to the Protestant faith.

But the O'Connors of Connacht remained true to both their homeland and their faith – a determined stance that ultimately paid off when in 1787 Charles Owen O'Conor was able to build Clonalis House, near their ancient seat at Castlerea.

This new seat of the O'Connor sept known as O'Connor Don – with 'don' indicating 'brown' – is home today to not only a fascinating collection of historical documents, but also the ancient inauguration stone of the O'Connor kings of Connacht.

It was this sacred stone that formed an integral part of the ceremony known as Banais Rí, or the King's Marriage, when he would be symbolically 'married' to the soil of his territory.

The century that saw the O'Connor acquisition of

Clonalis House also saw the birth of a number of prominent Irish scholars, including the antiquarian Charles O'Conor, while his grandson Charles O'Conor, born in 1767, served as a president of the distinguished Royal Irish Academy.

One O'Connor who lived through particularly interesting times was Arthur O'Connor, born in 1763 near Bandon, in Co. Cork, and who died in 1852.

He not only campaigned for Ireland's independence as a member of the Society of United Irishmen, but also became a general in the army of France's Napoleon Bonaparte after travelling to Paris in 1804.

One of his nephews was the political campaigner Feargus O'Connor, who was born in 1794.

The founder in 1837 of the radical newspaper *The Northern Star*, O'Connor later became such a leading light of the political reform movement known as Chartism, that many Chartists actually named their children after him.

Among the many illegitimate children that the unmarried O'Connor himself fathered was the famous London stage actor and theatre owner Edward O'Connor Terry.

Elected as a British Member of Parliament for Nottingham, he was later certified a lunatic and committed to an asylum after insulting a fellow politician – and it was in these grim surroundings that he died in 1855.

Chapter four:

On the world stage

Bearers of the name of O'Connor have achieved fame and distinction in a wide range of pursuits.

Born in Chicago in 1925, **Donald O'Connor** was the American dancer, singer, and actor best known for his performance with Gene Kelly in the 1952 musical *Singin' in the Rain*. He died in 2003.

Also on the stage **Des O'Connor** is the popular British entertainer who was born to an Irish father and a Jewish mother in the Stepney area of London in 1932.

He has appeared at venues ranging from the famed London Palladium to the MGM Grand in Las Vegas, having first entered show business after completing his national service with the Royal Air Force.

Presently the host of the British television show *Countdown*, he has also enjoyed a successful career as a singer, recording more than thirty albums and selling more than 15 million records.

The veteran entertainer was presented in 2001 with the Special Recognition Award at the National Television Awards for his contributions to television.

Serving with the United States Merchant Marine during the Second World War, **John O'Connor** later became the successful actor who is probably best known for his television role as the bigoted American working man Archie Bunker.

Born in 1924 in the Bronx, New York, he worked for a time as a schoolteacher following his war service before embarking on an acting career.

The role that first made him famous was as Major General Colt in the 1970 movie *Kelly's Heroes*, while his television career began with the role of Archie Bunker in the 1970s sitcom *All in the Family* (an American adaptation of the British sitcom *Till Death Do Us Part*), followed by *Archie Bunker's Place*, that ran from 1979 to 1983.

The actor, who died in 2001, also starred in the television sitcoms *In the Heat of the Night* and, towards the end of his career, *Mad About You*.

Back across the ocean to Britain **Tom O'Connor**, born in 1939 in Bootle, Merseyside is the actor and comedian best known for presenting British television game shows such as *Crosswits*, *Gambit*, and *Name That Tune*.

Bearers of the name of O'Connor have also excelled, and continue to excel, in the highly competitive world of sport.

On the golf course **Christy O'Connor Snr.** is the Irish professional golfer who was born in 1924 in Knocktaker, Co. Galway.

Turning professional in 1946, he helped his native Ireland to win the Canada Cup in 1958, while he played in the Ryder Cup from 1955 to 1973.

A six-times winner of the PGA Seniors Championship and of the World Senior Championship in 1976 and 1977, he is the uncle of the equally talented golfer **Christy O'Connor Jnr.**, who was born in 1948 in Co. Galway.

Turning professional in 1967, he has since won four European Tour events, two senior British Open titles, two Champions Tour Events, and played twice in the Ryder Cup. He is now also involved in golf course design.

On the baseball field **Daniel O'Connor**, born in 1868 in Guelph, Ontario, and who died in 1942, was the talented Major League Baseball first baseman who played for the Louisville Colonels of the American Association in 1890, while **Brian O'Connor**, born in 1977 in Cincinnati, is the retired American Major League Baseball pitcher who played for the Pittsburgh Pirates.

In the athletics arena **Peter O'Connor** was the noted Irish athlete who joined the Gaelic Association in 1896 and won the All-Ireland medals three years later in long jump, high jump, and triple jump.

Born in the north of England in 1872 but growing up in Ireland's Co. Wicklow, he later won a gold medal for the triple jump and a silver for the long jump in the 1906 Olympic Games in Athens.

Born in 1966 in St. Catherine, Jamaica, **Patrick O'Connor** is the retired Jamaican sprinter who took bronze in the 4 x 400-metres relay at the 1991 World Championships in Tokyo.

On the football pitch **Garry O'Connor**, born in Edinburgh in 1983, is the Scottish striker who, at the time of writing, plays for Birmingham City, while **James O'Connor**, born in 1979 in Dublin, is the Irish midfielder who won Player of the Year Award for 2002-2003 while playing for English club Stoke.

On the rugby pitch **Michael O'Connor**, nicknamed 'Snoz', is the leading Australian rugby league and rugby union player who was born in 1960 in Nowra, New South Wales, and who has represented his country in both rugby league and rugby union.

Born in 1962, **David O'Connor** is the American equestrian rider who takes part in eventing competitions and who won gold for his country at the 2000 Olympic Games in Sydney.

At the time of writing only the second American to have won Britain's Badminton Horse Trials, he is also president of the U.S. Equestrian Federation.

His wife is fellow equestrian **Karen O'Connor**, who was born Karen Lende in 1958 in Massachusetts.

Winner of the silver medal for the three-day team event at the 1996 Olympics in Atlanta, she took bronze at the 2000 Olympics and gold at the Pan American Games in Rio de Janeiro in 2007 for team eventing and gold for individual eventing.

From sport to music, **Mark O'Connor** is the internationally renowned fiddler who was born in 1961 in

Seattle, Washington, and who was named Musician of the Year by the Country Music Association every year from 1991 to 1996.

He is also the recipient of two Grammy Awards – one for his album *New Nashville Cats* and one for *Appalachian Journey*.

Born in Coventry in 1955 **Hazel O'Connor** is the British actress, singer, and songwriter who both starred in, and wrote the soundtrack for, the 1980 film *Breaking Glass*.

This won her a Variety Club of Great Britain Award for Best Film Actor and BAFTA nominations for Best Newcomer and Best Film Score.

In 2005 she released the equally critically acclaimed *Hidden Heart* album.

Across the sea to Ireland **Sinéad O'Connor**, is the highly talented but often controversial singer, songwriter, and musician who was born in Dublin in 1966.

She first came to international attention in 1990 with the release of *Nothing Compares 2 U*, which received Grammy nominations that included Record of the Year and Best Female Pop Vocal Performance and the award for Best Alternative Music Performance.

She was at the centre of controversy in 1992 after tearing up a photograph of Pope John II while on America's *Saturday Night Live* television show, in protest over alleged abuse of children by the Roman Catholic Church.

She later apologised for her actions and continues to

enjoy success not only as a solo performer, but also as a collaborator with fellow musicians such as Peter Gabriel and U2.

In the world of books her brother **Joseph O'Connor**, born in 1963, is the Irish novelist and former journalist whose 1991 novel *Cowboys and Indians* was short-listed for the prestigious Whitbread prize.

In the equally creative world of art **William Conor**, was the gifted artist who was born in Belfast in 1884 and who died in 1968.

Saving his meagre earnings from work as a manual labourer in his native city, he was able to study art in both Dublin and Paris and later returned to Belfast where his gifted brush recorded the everyday lives of the city's mill and shipyard workers.

Once asked why he spelled his name with only one 'n', he replied with typical Irish wit that it was because 'he could never make Ns meet.'

On the field of battle **Luke O'Connor**, born in 1831 at Elphin, Co. Roscommon, holds the distinction of having been the first soldier to be awarded the Victoria Cross – the highest award for gallantry for British and Commonwealth forces.

He had been aged 23 and a sergeant in the 23rd Regiment, British Army, during the Crimean War when he took part in the battle of the Alma in September of 1854.

Advancing between two officers and carrying the

regiment's colours, he was shot but managed to continue his advance as men fell all around him.

Later achieving the rank of Major General, he died in 1915.

Born in 1889 in Srinagar, India, **General Sir Richard O'Connor** was the distinguished British Army general who was highly decorated for his actions during the Second World War.

Commander of the Western Desert Force in the early years of the war, he was later captured but managed to escape and went on to command a Corps in the aftermath of the Normandy invasion of June 1944.

He died in 1981.

Taking to the skies **Bryan O'Connor**, born in 1946 in Orange, California, is the retired United States Marine Corps colonel and former NASA astronaut who, at the time of writing, serves as NASA's chief safety and mission assurance officer.

Key dates in Ireland's history from the first settlers to the formation of the Irish Republic:

circa 7000 B.C.	Arrival and settlement of Stone Age people.
circa 3000 B.C.	Arrival of settlers of New Stone Age period.
circa 600 B.C.	First arrival of the Celts.
200 A.D.	Establishment of Hill of Tara, Co. Meath, as seat of the High Kings.
circa 432 A.D.	Christian mission of St. Patrick.
800-920 A.D.	Invasion and subsequent settlement of Vikings.
1002 A.D.	Brian Boru recognised as High King.
1014	Brian Boru killed at battle of Clontarf.
1169-1170	Cambro-Norman invasion of the island.
1171	Henry II claims Ireland for the English Crown.
1366	Statutes of Kilkenny ban marriage between native Irish and English.
1529-1536	England's Henry VIII embarks on religious Reformation.
1536	Earl of Kildare rebels against the Crown.
1541	Henry VIII declared King of Ireland.
1558	Accession to English throne of Elizabeth I.
1565	Battle of Affane.
1569-1573	First Desmond Rebellion.
1579-1583	Second Desmond Rebellion.
1594-1603	Nine Years War.
1606	Plantation' of Scottish and English settlers.
1607	Flight of the Earls.
1632-1636	Annals of the Four Masters compiled.
1641	Rebellion over policy of plantation and other grievances.
1649	Beginning of Cromwellian conquest.
1688	Flight into exile in France of Catholic Stuart monarch James II as Protestant Prince William of Orange invited to take throne of England along with his wife, Mary.
1689	William and Mary enthroned as joint monarchs; siege of Derry.
1690	Jacobite forces of James defeated by William at battle of the Boyne (July) and Dublin taken.

1691	Athlone taken by William; Jacobite defeats follow at Aughrim, Galway, and Limerick; conflict ends with Treaty of Limerick (October) and Irish officers allowed to leave for France.
1695	Penal laws introduced to restrict rights of Catholics; banishment of Catholic clergy.
1704	Laws introduced constricting rights of Catholics in landholding and public office.
1728	Franchise removed from Catholics.
1791	Foundation of United Irishmen republican movement.
1796	French invasion force lands in Bantry Bay.
1798	Defeat of Rising in Wexford and death of United Irishmen leaders Wolfe Tone and Lord Edward Fitzgerald.
1800	Act of Union between England and Ireland.
1803	Dublin Rising under Robert Emmet.
1829	Catholics allowed to sit in Parliament.
1845-1849	The Great Hunger: thousands starve to death as potato crop fails and thousands more emigrate.
1856	Phoenix Society founded.
1858	Irish Republican Brotherhood established.
1873	Foundation of Home Rule League.
1893	Foundation of Gaelic League.
1904	Foundation of Irish Reform Association.
1913	Dublin strikes and lockout.
1916	Easter Rising in Dublin and proclamation of an Irish Republic.
1917	Irish Parliament formed after Sinn Fein election victory.
1919-1921	War between Irish Republican Army and British Army.
1922	Irish Free State founded, while six northern counties remain part of United Kingdom as Northern Ireland, or Ulster; civil war up until 1923 between rival republican groups.
1949	Foundation of Irish Republic after all remaining constitutional links with Britain are severed.